SACRED HEAVENS

Coloring Experiences for the Mystical and Magical

Illustrations by
LYDIA HESS

HARPER**ELIXIR**
An Imprint of HarperCollinsPublishers

This book is dedicated to my family.
My Leo husband, Robbie, for his steadfast
support and encouragement; and my two
Sagittarius daughters, Tucker and Aubrey,
for their creative consultations.

SACRED HEAVENS. Copyright © 2016 HarperCollins Publishers. Illustrations © 2016 by Lydia Hess.
All rights reserved. Printed in the United States of America. No part of this book may be used
or reproduced in any manner whatsoever without written permission except in the case of brief quotations
embodied in critical articles and reviews. For information address HarperCollins Publishers,
195 Broadway, New York, NY 10007.

HarperCollins books may be purchased for educational, business, or sales promotional use.
For information please e-mail the Special Markets Department at SPsales@harpercollins.com.

HarperCollins website: http://www.harpercollins.com

FIRST EDITION
Designed by Lydia Hess
Library of Congress Cataloging-in-Publication Data is available upon request.
ISBN 978–0–06–256364–4

16 17 18 19 20 BRR 10 9 8 7 6 5 4 3 2 1

Welcome to Sacred Heavens.
As you set out on an illuminating
journey that bridges worlds both
within and without, we invite you to contemplate the
celestial mysteries embodied in these images. From ancient
times, dreamers and seekers have looked to the night sky and
sought guidance in the stars, imbuing the heavenly constellations
with wisdom from the symbols, myths, and archetypes of our
oldest stories. From that ancestral wisdom emerged the twelve
signs of the Zodiac and the tradition of astrology, linking the
travels of the sun, moon, and the planets to the earth and
all living things: as above, so below. Our hope is that as
you color your way through these sacred heavens,
your mind quiets and your everyday cares
recede as your soul expands.

LYDIA HESS

The Zodiac

Aries ♈

Taurus ♉

Gemini ♊

Cancer ♋

Leo ♌

Virgo ♍

Libra ♎

Scorpio ♏

Sagittarius ♐

Capricorn ♑

Aquarius ♒

Pisces ♓

The Planets

Sun

Moon

Mercury

Venus

Mars

Jupiter

Saturn

Uranus

Neptune

Pluto

Fire Signs

passionate · independent · spontaneous

Aries

Leo

Sagittarius

Aries

[*March 21 – April 19*]

The Ram

courageous

generous

enthusiastic

optimistic

Leo

[*July 23 — August 22*]

The Lion

ambitious

generous

confident

creative

Sagittarius

[*November 22 – December 21*]

The Archer

upbeat

entertainer

adventurous

confident

Fire Sign Ruling Planets

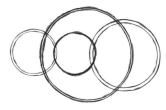

Aries • Mars

Leo • Sun

Sagittarius • Jupiter

Mars • Sun • Jupiter

Fire Sign Botanicals

Aries • Tomato

Leo • Sunflower

Sagittarius • Honeysuckle

Tomato • Sunflower • Honeysuckle

Earth Signs

grounded • responsible • sensual

Taurus

Virgo

Capricorn

Taurus

[April 20 – May 20]

The Bull

generous

loyal

friendly

reliable

Virgo
[August 23 – September 22]

The Maiden

reliable

intelligent

helpful

organized

Capricorn
[December 22 – January 19]

Capricorn

The Goat

♑

humorous

ambitious

caring

sympathetic

Earth Sign
Ruling Planets

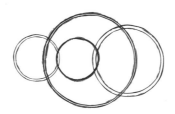

Taurus • Mercury

Virgo • Venus

Capricorn • Saturn

Mercury · Venus · Saturn

Earth Sign Botanicals

Taurus • Foxglove

Virgo • Lavender

Capricorn • Aspen

♉   ♍   ♑

Foxglove · Lavender · Aspen

Air Signs

curious • witty • brilliant

Gemini

Libra

Aquarius

Gemini

[May 21 – June 20]

The Twins

energetic

clever

imaginative

independent

Libra

[September 23 — October 22]

The Scales

peaceful

graceful

romantic

sociable

Aquarius

[January 20 – February 18]

The Water Bearer

inventive

original

humanitarian

visionary

Air Sign
Ruling Planets

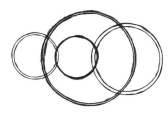

Gemini • Mercury

Libra • Venus

Aquarius • Uranus

Mercury · Venus · Uranus

Air Sign
Botanicals

Gemini • Rose

Libra • Daisy

Aquarius • Citrus

Rose • Daisy • Citrus

Water Signs

creative • empathetic • observant

Cancer

Scorpio

Pisces

Cancer

[June 21 – July 22]

Cancer

The Crab

sympathetic

caring

intelligent

imaginative

Scorpio

[*October 23 – November 21*]

The Scorpion

♏

passionate

dynamic

resourceful

intuitive

Pisces

[February 19 – March 20]

Pisces

The Fish

adaptable

devoted

loyal

compassionate

LYDIA HESS

Water Sign
Ruling Planets

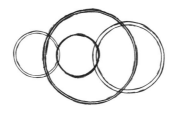

Cancer • Moon

Scorpio • Pluto

Pisces • Neptune

Moon · Pluto · Neptune

Water Sign Botanicals

Cancer • Water Lily

Scorpio • Onion

Pisces • Willow

♋ ♏ ♓

Water Lily · Onion · Willow

The End